MARINE CONSERVATION

BY CAROL HAND

Essential Library

An Imprint of Abdo Publishing
abdobooks.com

ABDOBOOKS.COM

Published by Abdo Publishing, a division of ABDO, PO Box 398166, Minneapolis, Minnesota 55439. Copyright © 2025 by Abdo Consulting Group, Inc. International copyrights reserved in all countries. No part of this book may be reproduced in any form without written permission from the publisher. Essential Library™ is a trademark and logo of Abdo Publishing.

Printed in the United States of America, North Mankato, Minnesota.

052024
092024

Cover Photo: Nico Faramaz/Shutterstock Images
Interior Photos: Petr Tran/Shutterstock Images, 4; Andriy Nekrasov/Shutterstock Images, 7; Shutterstock Images, 9, 12, 46, 51, 52, 69, 75, 84, 92, 97; Felix Nendzig/Shutterstock Images, 14–15; Nicole Helgason/Shutterstock Images, 16; Wolfgang Kaehler/LightRocket/Getty Images, 19; Jesus Cobaleda/Shutterstock Images, 22; Roger L. Wollenberg/UPI/Alamy, 25; Stely Nikolova/Shutterstock Images, 26; Nikita M. Production/Shutterstock Images, 28; Universal History Archive/Universal Images Group/Getty Images, 30; AP Images, 33; Phillip Colla/Blue Planet Archive, 36–37; Ethan Daniels/Shutterstock Images, 40; MDay Photography/Shutterstock Images, 44; Carl Court/Getty Images News/Getty Images, 48–49; Evgenii Parilov/Alamy, 54–55; Mohamed Abdulraheem/Shutterstock Images, 59; Peter Dejong/AP Images, 60; Luis Tato/AFP/Getty Images, 63; James Jones Jr./Shutterstock Images, 64; Wim Claes/Shutterstock Images, 67; Joost van Uffelen/Shutterstock Images, 72–73; Adisorn Chabsungnoen/SOPA Images/LightRocket/Getty Images, 76; Wan Faidz/Shutterstock Images, 78; Andreas Altenburger/Shutterstock Images, 81; Paul Chinn/San Francisco Chronicle/AP Images, 87; Robert F. Bukaty/AP Images, 89; Yuri Cortez/AFP/Getty Images, 90; Mike Aguilera/SeaWorld San Diego/Getty Images Entertainment/Getty Images, 98; Krzysztof Odziomek/Shutterstock Images, 101

Editor: Haley Williams
Series Designer: Cynthia Della-Rovere

Library of Congress Control Number: 2023949596

PUBLISHER'S CATALOGING-IN-PUBLICATION DATA
Names: Hand, Carol, author.
Title: Marine conservation / by Carol Hand
Description: Minneapolis, Minnesota: Abdo Publishing, 2025 | Series: Protecting our planet | Includes online resources and index.
Identifiers: ISBN 9781098293451 (lib. bdg.) | ISBN 9798384912729 (ebook)
Subjects: LCSH: Marine resources conservation--Juvenile literature. | Restoration ecology--Juvenile literature. | Conservation of natural resources--Juvenile literature. | Marine biodiversity conservation--Juvenile literature. | Environmental sciences--Juvenile literature.
Classification: DDC 333.951--dc23

CONTENTS

Approximately 9.2 million people
visited the islands of Hawaii in 2022.

BECOMING AN OCEAN ADVOCATE

Tyler was thoroughly enjoying his vacation. He was finally visiting Hawaii for the first time. To a teen from Nebraska, Hawaii was like another world. It had constant warm breezes, mountains, palm trees, and impossibly blue water. The tide would cover the white sand beaches and then recede, leaving behind shells and seaweed along with tide pools filled with tiny fish, snails, and hermit crabs. Best of all were the beautiful waves, with tanned surfers effortlessly riding them onto shore.

Tyler's family did all the touristy things, including watching whales and sea turtles, snorkeling over coral reefs, and visiting volcanoes. Tyler even took surfing lessons. But the final part of the trip promised to be different.

"You're seeing all the beautiful parts of Hawaii," his dad said. "But you need to see the rest of it, too. People are polluting and destroying Hawaii's beauty, and they're killing some of its most important wildlife. We need to stop this, but first, we have to know what's happening."

VIEWING THE DAMAGE

That day, Tyler and his family learned about some of the effects pollution had on Hawaii's ocean and wildlife. First, they took a wildlife tour. Kai, their tour leader, took them on a short boat ride to see Hawaiian monk seals.

Kai explained that the seals were among the world's most endangered animals, with only around 1,600 remaining in the wild.[1] Many seals died every year from getting stuck in fishing lines, being entangled by plastic pollution, or starving from a lack of food. A related species, the Mediterranean monk seal, was even more endangered, and another species, the Caribbean monk seal, was classified as extinct.

"These are only a few of the many endangered marine animals," Kai told Tyler and his family. "Pollution, both liquid and solid waste, is threatening many species in Hawaii and elsewhere in the world."

In the afternoon, Tyler's family went snorkeling again.

This time, the reef they visited was not beautiful, clean, and filled with life. Instead, some of the coral branches were brown, broken, and covered with dark strands of slimy algae. Others were white and dead.

There were few fish swimming among the coral, and no crabs, sea stars, or sea slugs were crawling over the bottom of the ocean floor. Much of the water's surface was covered with brown sediment, almost like a layer of soil. Trash was scattered around, including empty drink bottles, plastic six-pack rings, and even plastic bags.

Worldwide, 37 percent of sharks and rays, 33 percent of reef corals, and 26 percent of mammals, including marine mammals, are threatened with extinction.[2]

Less than 1 percent of plastic pollution floats on the ocean's surface. The rest is usually found deeper in the water.

After the snorkeling tour, Leilani, their tour leader, explained what they had seen. She said the white, or bleached, corals were a result of global warming. High temperatures and increased acid from dissolved carbon dioxide were killing the coral. But much of the damage was due to direct human action. Reef visitors broke off pieces, sometimes literally sitting or walking on the corals. Also, pollution caused by Hawaii's many tourists ended up in the water. Even the sunscreen used by swimmers was toxic to corals.

Back onshore, Tyler and his family walked through one of Hawaii's most polluted beaches. Unlike the pristine white sand beaches Tyler had seen so far, this beach was closed because it was covered with trash. He discovered from Leilani that three of the world's most polluted beaches were in Hawaii. They were polluted by more than just trash, though. Inland cesspools also deposited their untreated wastewater onto the beaches. "Tomorrow," Leilani said, "you'll get a chance to help clean up Hawaii's beaches, at least a little."

MAKING A START

The next morning, Tyler was ready. Yesterday's revelations about Hawaii's pollution and its effects on wildlife had horrified him, and he wanted to do something to help. He and his parents met the rest of the cleanup crew on the beach they had seen yesterday. There were approximately 30 volunteers, with most members coming from a local organization known as the Surfrider Foundation. The organization worked to protect the

world's beaches and oceans. A few volunteers, including Tyler's family, were tourists. They all received reusable gloves and wore nontoxic sunscreen.

The work was hot and dirty but satisfying. As he worked, Tyler became more and more determined to help stop the pollution affecting Hawaii. Tyler decided to team up with Jennie, a girl about his age who was a tourist from Ohio. They picked up all kinds of trash, including six-pack rings, Styrofoam cups, plastic bottles, drinking straws, chunks of glass, flip-flops, and lost electronic devices such as earbuds and cell phones. There were even a couple of huge fishing nets. The nets were big, so Tyler and Jennie had to get help to dig them out of the sand and carry them to the trash-collection bags.

During their morning and afternoon cleanup sessions, the crew collected almost 1,500 pounds (680 kg) of garbage. As he watched another crew separate and categorize the trash, Tyler saw that a large percentage of it was plastic. He also realized that as much as his group had cleaned up today, it represented only a tiny amount of the total problem.

Tyler thought of all the hundreds of beaches in Hawaii and the thousands around the world. Many of them were polluted with plastics and other items people had unthinkingly discarded as waste. All that waste would enter the oceans and could injure or kill not only monk seals but other marine animals as well. Tyler wondered if there was a solution to this problem.

SAVING THE OCEANS FROM HOME

By the time he returned home to Nebraska, Tyler had a new cause. He couldn't stop thinking about the monk seals, the other endangered species he'd learned about, and the destruction and death on the coral reef. Surely he could help somehow, even from Nebraska.

Tyler had exchanged contact information with his tour guide friends, Kai and Leilani, so he could easily ask them questions about marine conservation efforts. He also had a phone number for his new friend Jennie. At home, Tyler enlisted his biology teacher from last year, his good friends, and his girlfriend, Emma, to take part in helping marine animals and the world's oceans.

For the entire next school year, Tyler became a marine conservation advocate. His small group, with help from their teacher, started a marine conservation club. They gave presentations at school and in the community to teach everyone about endangered marine species and how every person, even those who don't live by the ocean, contributed to problems affecting the ocean and marine life. At first, some people wondered how they could actually help. "We're in Nebraska," one student said. "What can we do about oceans from here?"

Tyler turned that question over to Kai, who spoke to them from Hawaii over a video call. "You can still be a great help to marine animals, even from the middle of the United States," Kai said. "You can join marine organizations working to save marine organisms and ecosystems. You can take care of your own rivers.

Most Endangered Marine Animals

A small dolphin known as the vaquita is one of the most endangered marine animals in the world. The vaquita lives only in Mexico's Gulf of California. In 2022, the IUCN Red List found only 18 vaquitas in the wild.[4] Another highly endangered marine species is the North Atlantic right whale, which had only 356 individuals remaining in the wild in 2022.[5] Other marine species that are threatened with extinction include Hawaiian monk seals, Kemp's ridley turtles, hawksbill turtles, and giant manta rays.

Researchers have estimated that around 80 percent of plastics that end up in the ocean come from 1,000 rivers across the world.

Remember, most rivers run into an ocean. Any pollution that enters your river will most likely enter the ocean. And one of the most helpful things we can all do is cut back on plastic use. Stop using single-use plastics, such as straws and plastic cups."

Programs to teach people about the problems were just the beginning. Soon, Tyler's growing club had a website, a blog, and plenty of TikTok posts. But it also looked for more hands-on ways to help. There were no chapters of the Surfrider Foundation in Nebraska, but Tyler found a local group that cleaned rivers and streams. The club started doing monthly cleanups along the Platte River and the Missouri River near Omaha.

On the first of these cleanups, Emma said, "Ew, this is disgusting! I can't believe people just leave their trash like this. Haven't they ever heard of garbage cans?"

They were cleaning up a section of the Platte River near a campground. Along the whole area, they found plastic water bottles, soda cans, containers for sunscreen and insect repellent, and plenty of paper and plastic food containers. Some people had apparently left their campsites without cleaning up at all.

Tyler looked around. He shook his head. "Yeah, if we don't clean this up, all of it will end up in the Missouri River, then the Mississippi, and then the Gulf of Mexico."

After their first cleanup, the club arranged to join the local group for some more cleanups. But based on their firsthand experience, Tyler and the rest of the club wanted to do more. They identified two organizations committed to cleaning up

4ocean

4ocean is a corporation working to clean up plastic and other trash from the world's oceans, rivers, and coastlines. It has 12 locations across Florida, Guatemala, and Indonesia. Since 2017, the corporation has picked up more than 17,000 short tons (15,000 metric tons) of trash.[6] Along with picking up trash, 4ocean makes bracelets out of recyclable materials. Some of the proceeds from the bracelets are then used to fund ocean cleanup projects and marine conservation efforts. Alex Schulze, cofounder of 4ocean, said, "It's our opportunity to do something now to have a better future for everybody."[7]

ocean plastics, which were the Ocean Cleanup and the Ocean
Blue Project. Then, the club set up a semester-long fundraising
project and turned it into a competition with Tyler's friend
Jennie and her high school in Ohio. Tyler's high school won.
Together, the two schools raised nearly $5,000, which they split
between their chosen plastic-fighting organizations. Tyler and
his committed group of young marine conservationists were
determined to do even more the next school year.

Along with the club, Tyler was already thinking further ahead to what he wanted to do as a career. He knew he wanted to study ocean conservation in college. Maybe he would even go to college in Hawaii. He would work to save the monk seals, whales, dolphins, and other endangered marine species. Tyler couldn't believe people could let such magnificent animals just die out. He vowed to spend the rest of his life saving them.

Scientists sometimes scuba dive
to study marine life up close.

THE SCIENCE OF MARINE CONSERVATION

The world's oceans are vast, comprising more than 70 percent of Earth's surface and 97 percent of all water on Earth.[1] Many people throughout history have assumed that oceans are essentially limitless because of their vast size. This meant many thought oceans could never be polluted, their habitats couldn't be destroyed, and their resources couldn't be depleted. Therefore, people didn't think they had to worry about how much waste was being dumped into the ocean or how many fish and other resources were being removed. However, they assumed wrong.

Marine conservation, also called ocean conservation, is the protection of the marine species and ecosystems in Earth's seas. Efforts to conserve the world's oceans include restoring marine areas, protecting marine animal populations, understanding the effects of human actions on the ocean, and mitigating the effects of climate change. Multiple scientific disciplines are involved in these efforts.

THE SCIENCE OF OCEANOGRAPHY

A general term for the scientific study of oceans is *oceanography*. This interdisciplinary field is sometimes divided into different subfields according to which type of science is most involved. These include biological, chemical, physical, and geological oceanography.

Biological oceanographers and marine biologists study ocean life. They look at the number of organisms in an area along with their life cycles, development, adaptations, and interactions with each other and with their environment. Chemical oceanographers and marine chemists are most concerned with the study of seawater. This includes the properties, composition, cycles, and interactions of seawater with the atmosphere and seafloor. Chemical oceanography is also extremely important in understanding the effects of ocean pollution, including the effects of toxic chemicals in seawater.

Physical oceanography includes the study of the physical processes of oceans, such as waves, tides, currents,

and gyres. It includes the study of beach erosion, the interactions of oceans and the atmosphere, and the movement of light and sound through water. Geological oceanography and marine geology involve the study of the ocean floor and the processes that form it. This includes the study of seafloor spreading, plate tectonics, and ocean circulation.

Rebecca Jackson is an oceanographer and professor at Rutgers University. From 2016 to 2018, Jackson conducted research on melting glaciers in Greenland and Alaska. She looked at the underwater melting of glaciers, known as submarine melting, and how that could affect the circulation of ocean water. To do this, unmanned kayaks were used to get close to dangerous glacial areas so measurements of melting glaciers could be safely taken.

During her research, Jackson found that submarine melting was happening at a faster rate than scientists had previously believed. And the next step in her research was to figure out why these melt rates were higher. "Our goal is to . . . work toward developing a better theory to predict melt rates based on ocean conditions. Ultimately, this is a critical step toward accurate modeling of ocean-glacier interactions and projections of sea level rise in the future," said Jackson.[3]

Scientists calculate that between 2000 and 2019, glaciers around the world lost about 294 billion short tons (267 billion metric tons) of ice per year.[4]

THE SCIENCE OF MARINE BIOLOGY

Many marine problems relate to life in the oceans and therefore rely heavily on biology, including biological oceanography and marine conservation biology, for their solutions. These problems include maintaining sustainable fisheries, preserving marine biodiversity, protecting and restoring threatened and endangered species, and dealing with invasive species in marine habitats. Scientists dealing with these problems must understand and employ a knowledge of life histories, population biology, and the ecology of various ocean environments.

Peter Etnoyer is a marine conservation scientist. Etnoyer works for the Center for Coastal Environmental Health and Biomolecular Research at the National Oceanic and Atmospheric Administration (NOAA). His job is to find areas in the ocean where life is abundant and healthy, known as sweet spots. He then works with governments and nonprofit organizations to make plans for protecting those ocean environments. Etnoyer has also worked to protect coral reefs, seamounts, and open-ocean habitats.

THE SCIENCE OF CLIMATE CHANGE

The term *climate change* describes a long-term change in average weather patterns. It can result from either natural or

human causes. But since the 1950s, virtually all climate change has been caused by human activity, mainly fossil fuel burning and deforestation. Fossil fuel burning releases heat-trapping greenhouse gases (GHGs) into the atmosphere, causing increased air and ocean temperatures. Deforestation reduces the number of trees performing photosynthesis, a natural process that removes carbon dioxide, a GHG, from the atmosphere. Burning fossil fuels and deforestation both cause global warming, a major aspect of climate change. Global warming is the rise in Earth's temperatures due to higher amounts of GHGs in the planet's atmosphere.

Since the late 1800s, the planet's average temperature has increased about 1.8 degrees Fahrenheit (1°C).[5] And global temperatures have continued to rise even more since the mid-1900s. Two-thirds of Earth's warming has occurred since 1975, with temperatures rising almost 0.4 degrees Fahrenheit (0.2°C) per decade.[6] Some local temperature changes may be explained by natural causes, but average global increases cannot.

Climate change affects many marine species, especially lobsters, crabs, clams, and corals.

Earth's global temperature is based on the amount of solar radiation absorbed by the planet compared with the amount reflected back into space. These amounts are determined by the concentration of GHGs in Earth's atmosphere. GHGs absorb solar radiation, or heat, holding it in the atmosphere rather than allowing it to reflect back into space. These gases include water vapor, carbon dioxide, methane, nitrous oxide, and ozone.

Balanced levels of atmospheric GHGs are essential to keeping Earth's temperature warm enough to support life. This is known as the greenhouse effect. However, in recent history, human activities have unbalanced GHGs in Earth's atmosphere. Rising GHG levels are occurring due to emissions from factories, farming, vehicles, and other sources, resulting in global warming. The consequences of global warming include higher ocean temperatures, rising sea levels, and more acidic oceans.

> " I just can't bear the idea that future generations may not experience a coral reef. The mission is to start solving the problem, not just study it.[7] "
>
> —Ruth Gates, marine biologist, 2016

The science of climate change intersects with many fields of ocean science. For example, Ruth Gates was a marine biologist who specialized in the study of corals. She strongly advocated for the preservation of coral reefs around the world. In 2003, she founded the Gates Coral Lab at the Hawai'i Institute of Marine Biology to study these important ecosystems.

As a PhD student in the late 1980s, Gates discovered that increased water temperatures in Jamaica were causing coral in the area to turn white. Normally, tiny algae called zooxanthellae live in the tissues of coral, providing food that gives the coral its color. But when water temperatures are too warm, coral will push out the algae, causing the coral to turn white. This is known as coral bleaching. While bleaching does not immediately kill coral, it does cause more stress on the animal, which can eventually lead to its death.

Before Gates passed away in 2018, she was working to develop "super corals" that are genetically more resistant to coral bleaching and the effects of climate change. Along with that, she also took part in a 2017 documentary called *Chasing Coral*, which won several awards. Today, NOAA holds the Ruth D. Gates Coral Restoration Innovation Grants competition to honor Gates and help continue funding coral-restoration projects.

OTHER OCEAN ISSUES

The science of pollution also relates to many areas of oceanography. More than 80 percent of marine pollution comes from human actions on land.[8] A large amount of this is plastics, including plastics that are improperly manufactured or disposed of. Wherever on land the plastic or other pollutant is released, it may wash into streams, then rivers, and eventually into the oceans. From there, it can travel around the world in ocean currents.

CARL SAFINA

Carl Safina is a marine ecologist who received his PhD from Rutgers University. He is one of the world's most ardent marine conservationists. Safina was born in Brooklyn, New York, in 1955. His love for animals emerged early in his childhood and continued into his adulthood.

During his professional life, Safina has worked to further marine conservation efforts. His ocean-related projects include working to ban harmful fishing methods and improving fishery laws in the United States. Internationally, he has worked to improve management of shark and tuna fisheries and pass a United Nations (UN) fisheries treaty.

In addition to his fieldwork, Safina is a renowned conservation writer. His ocean-related books include *Song for the Blue Ocean* and *A Sea in Flames: The Deepwater Horizon Oil Blowout*. Safina also hosted a ten-part television series from 2012 to 2013 called *Saving the Ocean*. *Audubon* magazine, which focuses on subjects related to nature, listed him as one of its 100 Notable Conservationists of the Twentieth Century. And in 2011, the digital news site *Utne Reader* named him one of 25 Visionaries Changing the World.

In 2003, Carl Safina founded the Safina Center, an environmental organization that focuses on conservation efforts and combating climate change.

Other forms of pollution include land runoff from agricultural or urban areas, oil spills, and ocean dumping. The pollutant could be anything from industrial waste to sewage to deliberate discharges from oil tankers and other ships. Much of this pollution is toxic. It kills organisms and harms marine ecosystems. The dumping of sewage and agricultural fertilizers adds excess nutrients to the water. This causes a process called eutrophication. The result is out-of-control algae growth, which lowers oxygen levels in the water, leading to the deaths of marine animals in bays, estuaries, and other environments near shorelines.

Pollution occurs in all types of marine ecosystems. It can also occur at all latitudes, from the Arctic to temperate to tropical waters. Ocean dumping of different materials, including sewage, industrial waste, garbage, chemicals, and other debris, has been a global problem for many years. Much of this occurs in coastal areas, but ships also sometimes dump garbage and chemicals into the open ocean. The mining industry alone is known to dump 243 million short tons (220 million metric tons) of hazardous waste into the oceans and other bodies of water every year.[9]

No part of the ocean is free from the effects of pollution. However, because most pollution originates on land, coastal and shallow-water ecosystems bear the brunt of its effects. Ports and harbors, river deltas, estuaries, and bays are much shallower than the open ocean and become more concentrated with pollution. People highly trained in science, as well as government officials, organizations, and activists, are all needed to deal with marine conservation issues.

Introduction of Invasive Species

Invasive species are species that are not native to an area but are accidentally or purposefully introduced there. They can destroy habitats, change food webs, displace existing organisms, or introduce diseases to an ecosystem. Invasive species are a major cause of declining biodiversity in marine ecosystems because they tend to multiply rapidly and can disrupt an ecosystem's balance. One example of an invasive species is the zebra mussel, which was accidentally brought to North America on ships from Asia's Black and Caspian Seas. The zebra mussel has led to the decline and extinction of several mussel species in North America.

Only about 5 percent of Earth's oceans have been explored.

THE HISTORY OF MARINE CONSERVATION

People have studied oceans since coastal dwellers first began to venture into them. These people learned how waves, tides, currents, and storms affected their travels and how to catch fish for food. At first, these early explorers passed information down through generations by stories and legends. Around 850 BCE, naturalists and philosophers began to study oceans more systematically. By the 1400s and 1500s CE, explorers had built large ships and were traveling to new continents, gradually increasing their knowledge of the marine world.

EARLY MARINE BIOLOGY AND OCEANOGRAPHY

HMS *Beagle* left England in 1831 to assist marine navigation by mapping the South American coastline. The British ship carried a young naturalist, Charles Darwin, who observed the adaptations of life both in the ocean and on land throughout the voyage. Based on his studies, Darwin eventually proposed theories about evolution that are still accepted today, with some minor changes.

The *Beagle*'s five-year voyage was one of the earliest to expand human knowledge of marine biology and geology.

The *Challenger* expedition was considered the beginning of modern oceanography. From 1872 to 1876, ocean studies were conducted from HMS *Challenger*, a British warship. Led by Canadian naturalist John Murray and Scottish naturalist Charles Wyville Thompson, this worldwide scientific expedition collected data on ocean temperatures, ocean currents, seawater chemistry, seafloor geology, and marine life.

Beginning in the 1930s, ocean exploration took a leap forward when people developed new technology to explore the deep oceans. The bathysphere, invented by Americans William Beebe and Otis Barton, was a spherical steel structure with room for people inside. Portholes allowed people to look outside the vessel.

More than 4,700 new plant and animal species were discovered during the *Challenger* expedition.

The bathysphere allowed people to dive deeper into the ocean than they had before. Beebe and Barton broke records in 1934 when they descended 3,028 feet (923 m) beneath the ocean surface.[1] Beebe's books detailing his observations of deep-sea life inspired many present-day marine biologists and oceanographers.

Other technologies for deep-ocean exploration were developed during and after World War II (1939–1945) when the US Navy saw a need to improve ocean warfare. This led to advances in submarines and the development of sonar. Sonar is used to help measure the depths of the ocean.

In 1960, a deep-sea submersible called *Trieste* completed a dive to the deepest known point in all the oceans, which is known as the Challenger Deep. The Challenger Deep is located in the Pacific Ocean's Mariana Trench. Swiss engineer Jacques Piccard and US Navy lieutenant Don Walsh traveled 35,813 feet (10,916 m) below sea level into Challenger Deep.[2]

During the 1960s, three types of underwater research vehicles were developed. They are human-occupied vehicles, remotely operated vehicles, and autonomous underwater vehicles. These vehicles continue to be used to this day, and each one has a specific role in deep-ocean research.

PEOPLE IN MARINE CONSERVATION

Often, the people motivated to explore and understand the oceans were so enthralled by this world that they became ardent marine conservationists. These scientists and explorers wanted to share the wonders of the ocean with everyone. Scientists who became important marine conservationists include Rachel Carson and Sylvia Earle. Some explorers who were marine conservationists include Hans Hass and Jacques-Yves Cousteau.

American Rachel Carson is best known for her book *Silent Spring*, which is about the dangers of pesticides. But Carson, an aquatic biologist, was captivated by oceans and coasts. Between 1941 and 1955, she wrote a trilogy of best-selling

The Shark Lady

Eugenie Clark was born in New York in 1922. Known as the Shark Lady for her expertise on shark behavior, she did most of her research underwater. Clark conducted 72 submersible dives and more than 200 field research expeditions. In 1973, she discovered reef sharks sleeping underwater in caves in the Yucatán Peninsula. Clark authored 175 scientific papers and three books, and she founded Florida's Mote Marine Laboratory. She conducted her last dive at age 92.

books about the oceans. Her books were scientifically accurate but written in a simple way to better share her understanding of oceans with nonscientists. Carson fought for marine conservation causes throughout her life.

American Sylvia Earle says she began her oceanography career at the age of three when she was knocked off her feet by a wave. She eventually obtained a PhD in botany from Duke University and has spent decades exploring the ocean. Earle became a celebrity in the scientific community when she was selected by the Smithsonian Institution to conduct research while living

In 1970, Sylvia Earle led four other female scientists on a two-week project photographing and observing marine species near the US Virgin Islands.

in an underwater habitat. In 1979, having already made many submersible dives, she broke the world record for untethered deep diving at 1,250 feet (381 m).[3] Earle wore a special suit, called a JIM suit, designed to withstand deep-ocean pressures. Through 2023, her record hasn't been broken.

Austrian biologist Hans Hass and his wife, Lotte Hass, explored the oceans and made documentaries. In 1938, Hans created his own camera to take pictures and film underwater. As one of the first people to interact underwater with a sperm whale, he also made important advances in the study of marine animal behavior.

French explorer Jacques-Yves Cousteau, along with French engineer Émile Gagnan, invented an air tank system that later became the basis for modern scuba breathing gear. This helped Cousteau dive for longer and even film underwater. Cousteau produced the award-winning documentary *The Silent World* in 1956 and later starred in the 1977 PBS series *The Cousteau Odyssey*. His ocean documentaries won 40 Emmy awards, and he has inspired several generations to love and respect the oceans.

THE MARINE CONSERVATION MOVEMENT

In the 1960s and 1970s, people around the world started becoming more interested in environmental causes of all kinds. This included ocean conservation. During that time, it became more apparent that humans could damage oceans and that it was necessary to protect oceans and the species that lived there.

Cousteau's documentaries played a large part in this awakening. With the improvement of scuba diving technology, more people were able to experience undersea habitats, such as coral reefs, firsthand. Recordings of whale songs showed that whales were highly intelligent. This led to outcries against whaling, which eventually resulted in most countries banning it entirely.

Beginning in the 1970s, the United States passed laws to protect the oceans and marine life. In 1972, Congress passed the Marine Mammal Protection Act to prevent the extinction of various marine species, including whales, dolphins, porpoises, seals, sea lions, walruses, manatees, sea otters, and polar bears. NOAA Fisheries, the US Fish and Wildlife Service, and the Marine Mammal Commission share the responsibility for protecting these marine species.

Also in 1972, the National Marine Sanctuaries Act was passed. This act gave Congress or the executive branch the power to protect important marine ecosystems within a defined area using a specific management plan.

Further protection for marine mammals and other marine species, such as sharks, rays, and reef corals, was provided by the Endangered Species Act passed in 1973.

In 1972, Congress also passed a law known as the Marine Protection, Research, and Sanctuaries Act (MPRSA) to deal with the increasingly serious problem of ocean dumping. The MPRSA is enforced by the Environmental Protection Agency (EPA) and is better known as the Ocean Dumping Act. Its purpose is to prevent the dumping of materials that "would unreasonably degrade or endanger human health or the marine environment."[4]

In 1976, Congress passed the Magnuson-Stevens Fishery Conservation and Management Act (MSA) to prevent overfishing

> " Nothing is more priceless and more worthy of preservation than the rich array of animal life with which our country has been blessed.[5] "
>
> —Richard Nixon, US president, 1973

within federal waters. Over the years, other laws have been passed regarding the protection of certain species or specific aspects of the marine environment, such as maintaining clean water. Scientists are also developing methods to help conserve entire marine ecosystems and their biodiversity.

MARINE PROTECTED AREAS

Marine protected areas (MPAs) have become an important conservation effort to help protect the planet's oceans. MPAs are

legally protected places that are established to preserve the marine animals and habitats in that area. Human activities are regulated in these areas to maintain the natural environment and promote biodiversity.

Modern MPAs can trace their origins to the International Union for Conservation of Nature (IUCN). The IUCN World Parks Congress held its First World Conference on National Parks in 1962. During this conference, governments from around the world discussed the importance of establishing national parks and protected areas. This included the protection of marine environments.

Efforts to protect the ocean continued over the next few decades. In 1975, Australia passed the Great Barrier Reef Marine Park Act to protect and manage the largest coral reef system in the world, the Great Barrier Reef. By 1985, around 430 MPAs had been created.[6]

However, it wasn't until the 1992 Earth Summit in Rio de Janeiro, Brazil, that international agreements and regulations related to MPAs were more formally established. During the summit, an agreement known as the Convention on Biological Diversity (CBD) was formed, calling on countries to "establish a system of protected areas or areas where special measures need to be taken to conserve biological diversity."[7] Scientists also brought forth evidence at the Rio Earth Summit that overfishing was lowering the populations of many species of fish and destroying habitats.

In 2004, the CBD proposed that by 2012, 10 percent of the world's oceans needed to be protected to help increase global marine conservation efforts.[9] Since that goal was first established, the target date has been extended several times. Along with that, many countries have begun working toward higher MPA goals.

Over thousands of years, the concept of marine conservation biology has evolved from a few fishers trying to harvest food near the shore to scientists studying the ocean as a whole. Today, many parts of the ocean still remain a mystery, but it is apparent that human actions are continuously damaging this vital part of Earth. Since people cannot always see the effects of their actions, whole marine ecosystems are at risk of being destroyed.

Scientists believe coral reefs are one of
the most biodiverse ecosystems on Earth.

OCEANS AND CLIMATE CHANGE

Climate change has had a major effect on Earth's oceans. The ocean is a carbon sink, meaning it absorbs more carbon from the atmosphere than it releases into it. Due to human activities, increased levels of carbon and other greenhouse gases are being released into the atmosphere. This causes the planet to warm and oceans to absorb the excess carbon.

Higher GHG levels can take longer to affect the ocean than they do land. Even so, it is evident that oceans are getting warmer, sea levels are rising, and water is becoming more acidic. Many marine animals and habitats have already felt the effects of these changes, and they will continue to do so as long as climate change continues to be a problem.

HIGHER OCEAN TEMPERATURES

The oceans cover more than 70 percent of Earth's surface and have absorbed as much as 90 percent of the heat trapped by rising GHG levels.[1] Ocean temperatures are rising at all depths because of the tremendous amounts of heat being absorbed.

The greatest rate of increase in ocean temperatures is occurring at the ocean's surface to a depth of about 250 feet (76 m).[2] This is where most ocean organisms live, and many of them are extremely sensitive to even small temperature changes.

For example, marine heat waves have majorly affected many marine animals and ecosystems. Marine heat waves are periods of time when ocean surface temperatures in certain areas are higher than normal. The increased temperatures are identified by comparing past average ocean temperatures during the same time frame.

When an area of ocean experiences a heat wave, it means the ocean temperature is 90 percent warmer than in previous years.[3] Marine heat waves can last for weeks or months, or sometimes even years.

Since the 1970s, marine heat waves due to human activity have doubled in frequency.[4] They are now intensifying, lasting longer, and covering greater areas of the ocean. Between 2013 and 2017, a heat wave known as "the Blob" took over parts of the Pacific Ocean from off the coast of California up to Alaska. It was considered one of the worst marine heat waves ever recorded.

During that time, a decline in food sources led humpback whales to move closer to shore to feed. However, the areas near shore where the whales were feeding were commonly used by crab fisheries. This caused more whales to become tangled in nets, with 53 being caught in 2015 and 55 being caught in 2016.[5]

Another likely effect of rising ocean temperatures is the changing behavior of storms such as hurricanes and tropical cyclones. Due to higher temperatures and greater heat energy in the oceans, storm intensity in the Atlantic, Caribbean, and Gulf of Mexico has increased. Since 1980, scientists have found that the number of Category 3 and above hurricanes has doubled in the Atlantic Ocean.[6] Higher ocean temperatures cause these storms to pull more water vapor and heat into them, creating more powerful winds and increased amounts of rainfall. The enormous amounts of rain make coastal flooding more likely.

Also, these storms are moving at a much slower rate, meaning they can cause more damage in the areas they hit. While scientists don't expect the frequency of hurricanes to rise, models

Storing Heat

Oceans have a very high heat capacity compared with land. They are vital in storing the excess heat resulting from global warming, preventing Earth from warming as fast as it would otherwise. Since 1955, oceans have stored more than 90 percent of Earth's excess heat.[7] Heat is absorbed at the ocean surface but gradually moves down. Surface temperatures vary yearly due to changing weather conditions, but deeper temperatures are much less variable. These deeper temperatures have been steadily rising for decades.

have suggested that there is a greater chance Category 4 and 5 storms will occur, which are the highest categories of hurricanes. This means that with current ocean warming trends, these storms will only continue to become more intense and damaging.

Along with heat waves and more intense storms, rising ocean temperatures will cause the most damage to coastal and near-shore ecosystems, such as coral reefs and mangrove swamps. Between 1901 and 2020, ocean surface temperatures rose an average of 0.14 degrees Fahrenheit (0.08°C) every decade.[8] According to estimates from the United Nations (UN), a temperature increase of 2.7 degrees Fahrenheit (1.5°C) will destroy 70 to 90 percent of the planet's coral reefs. The UN also

Bleaching not only affects coral, but it also affects the many species that rely on coral for food and shelter.

predicts that an increase of 3.6 degrees Fahrenheit (2°C) will destroy nearly 100 percent of reefs.[9]

HIGHER SEA LEVELS

Rising sea levels, a major impact of global warming, occurs in two ways. First, water expands when it warms, taking up more space. This factor, known as thermal expansion, accounts for about half of the world's sea level rise since the late 1990s.[10] Second, water from melting ice sheets and glaciers runs into the ocean, adding more water. Increased air temperatures are causing the huge ice sheets covering

The ocean's mass has increased about 0.1 inches (0.2 cm) per year between 2002 and 2023, causing coastal sea levels to rise.[14]

both Greenland and Antarctica to melt more rapidly. Also, glaciers are melting more in the summers and are not replenishing as much in the winter because less snowfall is occurring.

Between 1880 and 2022, sea levels have increased on average about eight to nine inches (21–24 cm).[11] According to satellite measurements, the total rise between 1993 and 2022 was 3.6 inches (9.1 cm). And the rate of sea level rise is increasing every year. In 1993, the sea level rose 0.08 inches (0.20 cm). In 2022, it rose 0.17 inches (0.44 cm).[12] By 2050, sea levels are expected to rise about one foot (0.3 m) along US coastlines.[13]

On the US Atlantic Coast, sea level rise has caused beaches to narrow and some houses to be washed away. In some low-lying island countries, such as Tuvalu in the Pacific, dwellings have

submerged, and people had to evacuate to new locations. The Cook and Marshall Islands are also threatened. One island, called Majuro, has lost approximately 20 percent of its beaches.[15] Sea level rise in coastal areas can also cause erosion, flooding of wetlands, salt contamination of aquifers and soil, and loss of animal habitat.

Two important Arctic species threatened by melting ice are polar bears and harp seals. Harp seals provide food for polar bears. In 2019, nearly all the harp seal pups in Canada's Gulf of Saint Lawrence drowned because of melting ice, affecting the populations of both species.

In the United States, sea levels are rising fastest in the Gulf of Mexico, near the westward opening of the Mississippi River. The second-highest rate is occurring along the mid-Atlantic coast. Sea levels are currently falling in places such as Alaska, in part because melting glaciers are causing the land to rise. But even these areas will eventually have higher seas if atmospheric GHG levels continue to rise.

OCEAN ACIDIFICATION

Carbon dioxide, one of the most common GHGs, dissolves in ocean water. It reacts with the water to form carbonic acid. This increases the water's acidity. In the past 200 years, ocean acidity has increased by about 30 percent.[16]

Higher acid levels interfere with marine organisms' ability to create shells and skeletons, which are made of calcium carbonate. Affected organisms include sea stars, lobsters, crabs, some phytoplankton, and some mollusks. As ocean acidity increases further, the shells of these organisms begin to dissolve.

Coral is also affected by higher acidity. The entire structure of a coral reef is made of calcium carbonate, making it particularly vulnerable. As acid levels rise, the older coral skeletons at the

> It's probably fair to say that we have only begun understanding the extent to which climate change is going to wreak havoc on ocean health.[17]
>
> —Charlotte de Fontaubert, global lead for the World Bank's Blue Economy, 2022

47

bottom of the reef begin to dissolve. The foundation of the reef becomes weaker, and waves begin to erode it. New coral skeletons then have difficulty forming.

Greater acidity can also affect the behavior of certain kinds of fish. Some clown fish, for example, find it more difficult to detect predators in acidic waters. Young clown fish can have difficulty finding suitable habitats as well.

IMPLICATIONS FOR HUMANS

Warmer oceans lead to problems that affect people both directly and indirectly. On land, this includes flooding due to storms and rising sea levels along with coastal erosion. Within the water itself, higher ocean temperatures mean an increase in harmful algal blooms, more areas with lower levels of oxygen, higher death rates of marine mammals, a decline in fisheries, and more.

All these events are already happening and are expected to continue. In addition, more extreme weather events, such as storms, floods, and droughts, will affect many habitats and species, including humans. But the greatest effects on people are indirect. When climate change affects ocean health, it damages the ocean's ability to resist and relieve the effects of climate change.

Oceans are essential for life on Earth, and coastal ecosystems are vital for storing carbon from GHGs. The destruction of ecosystems such as mangroves, seagrasses, and salt marshes means the carbon dioxide they would have absorbed instead returns to the atmosphere or ocean. Mangroves store carbon dioxide up to four times faster than ecosystems on land. They also support fisheries, improve water quality, and protect coasts from storms and floods.

Coral reefs are equally valuable. They cover less than 0.1 percent of the world's oceans but support more than 25 percent of marine biodiversity. More than one billion people on Earth benefit from the

fisheries, coastal protection, medicines, and recreation that coral reefs provide.[18] But until steps are taken to reduce GHG emissions, coastal and marine environments, along with the people and organisms that live there, will continue to feel the effects of climate change.

Plastic bottles, straws, and bags are some of the most common waste found in oceans.

CHAPTER 5

OCEAN PLASTICS

A dead California gray whale washed up on the beach in 2010 in Puget Sound, Washington. Its stomach contained a pair of pants, a golf ball, towels, duct tape, surgical gloves, and more than 20 plastic bags. Plastic is not the only type of solid-waste pollution entering the oceans, but it does make up a majority of the waste found there.

Plastic is especially challenging as a pollutant because it is nearly indestructible. It does not break down chemically, so any plastic entering the environment remains there. Sunlight, wind, and currents break plastics into very tiny pieces. These pieces, known as microplastics, may contain toxins and are easily ingested by marine animals.

In 1950, 2.2 million short tons (2 million metric tons) of plastic was produced. By 2017, that increased to 384 million short tons (348 million metric tons).[1] Between 2000 and 2010, more plastic was produced than all the plastic made prior to the year 2000. Although totals are difficult to estimate, studies suggest that oceans now contain between 15 and 51 trillion pieces of plastic.[2]

SOURCES AND EFFECTS OF PLASTIC POLLUTION

Around 80 percent of marine debris comes from land. This includes trash, construction debris, and illegally dumped materials. Ports, marinas, and commercial and industrial facilities all contribute to marine debris. This waste material becomes urban runoff, or excess water that drains from outdoor structures, which eventually enters the oceans. The other 20 percent of marine debris is ocean based, such as discarded fishing gear, discharges from ships, and pollution from aquaculture.[3]

The most common type of solid waste comes from food containers and packaging, which account for 80 million short tons (73 million metric tons), or about 32 percent of total global waste, per year.[4] These pollutants, along with plastic bags, are among the largest components of marine debris. Food containers and packaging are particularly damaging because they are single-use items and therefore represent a major waste of resources.

Harm from plastics begins with production and continues after they've been used. Plastic is made from oil, which is a fossil fuel, and extracting oil from the ground can lead to environmental damage. It takes energy to turn oil into plastic, and generating that energy may release greenhouse gases.

When plastic products are discarded, they can have devastating effects on marine life and ecosystems. These products may suffocate, entangle, or injure animals. Animals may also eat them. The result may be infections, internal injuries, or death to the animals. Invasive species may also hitch rides on floating plastics, spreading them farther through marine ecosystems.

Plastics are everywhere in the environment, including in food chains. When people eat seafood, there is a chance they are also eating microplastics. These substances can have a variety of negative effects on the body. In addition, plastic pollution damages the economy through its effects on tourism, fisheries, and aquaculture.

PLASTICS VERSUS OCEAN WILDLIFE

Plastic pollution is a major problem for marine wildlife, especially when they ingest it. Animals may mistake plastics for food or ingest them accidentally. Microplastics travel invisibly throughout ocean food webs, but they can still harm marine life. Studies show that fish in the North Pacific eat 12,000 to 24,000 short tons (11,000–22,000 metric tons) of plastic annually. Some of this ingestion causes internal injuries and death, and some of it is transferred up the food chain to larger fish, mammals, and humans. A study of California markets showed that one-fourth of the fish had plastic, mainly microplastics, in their guts.[5]

Sea turtles often mistake floating plastic for food. They choke on it, suffer internal injuries, or starve to death because they feel full when their stomachs are filled with plastics. Half the world's sea turtles have ingested plastics, and their reproduction is being affected because of plastic pollution on beaches.[6]

Dead seabirds are often found with their stomachs filled with plastics. Estimates show that around 60 percent of all seabird species have ingested plastic. By 2050, experts believe this number will likely rise to 99 percent.[7] The problem is even worse for seabird chicks. Adult birds feed floating plastics to their babies, affecting growth and survival rates. One study showed that 98 percent of seabird chicks had plastics in them.[9]

Plastics cause another problem for sea turtles and for marine mammals, including whales, dolphins, seals, and sea lions. These animals breathe air. When they become entangled in large pieces of plastic, they may drown, starve, or suffer injuries and infections when the plastic cuts their flesh. Smaller animals drown quickly. Larger ones, such as whales, may drag the gear with them and eventually die of exhaustion. Entanglement is a major cause of human-caused deaths in humpback, right, and gray whales.

Scientists estimate that around 100,000 marine mammals die from plastic pollution annually.[11]

THE GREAT PACIFIC GARBAGE PATCH

Every year, around 1.3 to 2.7 million short tons (1.2 to 2.4 million metric tons) of plastic waste enter the oceans from rivers. More than half of it remains at the surface, where it is carried by currents.[10] Converging currents eventually deposit this plastic in the ocean's gyres, where it circulates as it is gradually worn down by waves and the sun.

The five major gyres are in the North and South Atlantic, the North and South Pacific, and the Indian Ocean. All five gyres have garbage patches. The largest, called the Great Pacific Garbage Patch, is in the Northern Pacific between California and Hawaii. The Great Pacific Garbage Patch covers

at least 618,000 square miles (1.6 million square km), which is twice the size of the state of Texas. It weighs an estimated 88,000 short tons (80,000 metric tons).[12] Due to seasonal changes in winds and currents, the exact location of the garbage patch is constantly changing.

The Great Pacific Garbage Patch is not a literal island of trash in the middle of the ocean. Instead, the trillions of plastic pieces are spread out over a large distance. "You can think of it like the

BOYAN SLAT

When Dutch student Boyan Slat was a teenager, he went scuba diving in Greece and saw more plastic bags than he did fish. He wondered why the bags couldn't just be cleaned up. Slat decided to do a project at school to develop technological methods for cleaning up ocean pollution.

At age 18, Slat started his nonprofit organization, the Ocean Cleanup. In 2012, he gave a presentation at a conference outlining his ideas, and the video quickly went viral. Using volunteers and a crowdfunding campaign, Slat undertook a yearlong study to further develop his technology.

Slat's system involves a slow-moving U-shaped barrier that creates an artificial coastline, which concentrates and collects ocean plastics using the power of currents. He also developed a smaller but similar system for cleaning rivers. In 2023, Slat marked his tenth year as chief executive officer (CEO) of the Ocean Cleanup. Many people didn't believe his technology was possible. Slat said, "When people say something is impossible, the sheer absoluteness of that statement should be a motivation to investigate further."[13]

In 2015, Boyan Slat was awarded the UN's Champions of the Earth Award, which honors those finding new ways to combat environmental threats.

night sky," says Matthias Egger from the Ocean Cleanup, which is an organization that develops technology to get rid of ocean plastics. "If you look up at night, you see all those white dots, that's essentially what you see in the garbage patch. It's not that dense, but there are a lot of them."[14]

A 2023 study described a new ecosystem existing on the trash in the Great Pacific Garbage Patch. Scientists identified 484 marine invertebrates from 46 different species living on the garbage patch. More than 80 percent of those species normally live on coasts. Dozens of coastal species, including small crabs and anemones, and open-ocean species are surviving and reproducing on individual pieces of trash in the Great Pacific Garbage Patch.[15] They have formed a new open-ocean ecosystem that has the potential to exist for years.

ATTEMPTS TO CONTROL PLASTIC POLLUTION

The current plastics economy is unsustainable. Plastic is entering the environment more rapidly every year. By 2050, given current rates, plastic pollution will likely outweigh all the fish in the oceans. Once plastic enters the oceans, it is extremely hard to remove. The best solution is to prevent plastics from entering oceans in the first place.

Many preventive solutions can start at the individual or small-group level. The most obvious is to reduce using single-use plastics. This solution requires paying attention to plastic use and forming new, environmentally sustainable habits. For example, plastic cups, plates, and bottles can be replaced with recyclable glass or metal ones, and plastic grocery bags can be replaced with reusable canvas bags. When plastics are used, they should be recycled properly to keep them out of oceans and to decrease the need for new plastics. By 2023, only about 9 percent of plastics were recycled around the world.[17]

Participation in beach or riverside cleanups is another method to keep plastics from entering oceans. Cleanups help prevent plastics from getting into the ocean to begin with. They can be done individually or through cleanups sponsored by local or international organizations, such as the Oceanic Society or the Ocean Conservancy.

People can also stay informed about the plastics problem, watch documentaries, and tell their friends. They can join and

In 2023, people protested in Kenya to express their want for an international treaty that will address plastic pollution.

support organizations dedicated to solving the ocean-plastics problem, including the Plastic Pollution Coalition, the 5 Gyres Institute, Algalita, and many others. Concerned citizens can support legislation designed to help with the issue, such as the 2021 Break Free from Plastic Pollution Act introduced by the US Senate. This act focuses on building strategies and policies for reducing plastic pollution in the United States. Although the bill had not passed through 2023, there are many state-level initiatives designed to hold plastic producers responsible for the pollution caused by the disposal of their products.

Fossil fuels account for more than 75 percent
of greenhouse gas emissions on Earth.

POLLUTION IN OCEAN ECOSYSTEMS

Ocean pollution endangers the health of both people and ecosystems. While plastic pollution is a huge issue, the invisible mix of chemicals, particles, metals, and biological toxins that come from other kinds of pollutants is just as concerning. The most toxic of these include thousands of industrial chemicals and the by-products of burning fossil fuels, especially coal. Climate change magnifies the pollution problem.

Chemical pollutants change ocean chemistry by causing acidification, adding excess nutrients, or poisoning the water. These pollutants are the greatest threat to shallow, near-shore habitats, but in some cases, their damage extends to the open ocean. Radioactive waste, noise, military sonar, and seafloor dredging in both shallow and deep-sea environments also threaten marine ecosystems.

POLLUTION FROM COASTAL ACTIVITIES

Poor land management is directly connected to ocean pollution. Human activities such as agriculture, deforestation, and construction can cause the erosion of soil, silt, and mud that then runs into rivers and eventually oceans. This radically changes or destroys ecosystems, resulting in extensive loss of biodiversity. Physical damage to the seafloor itself can occur because of some fishing practices and dropping boat anchors both in the open ocean and near the shore.

Dredging can also cause environmental problems. This process removes the entire top layer of an area of the seafloor, destroying ecosystems there. Dredging is done to maintain ship channels, ensuring that the water is deep enough for ships to safely travel.

Undersea mining is another activity that may threaten marine ecosystems. As people look for new sources of important minerals, there is growing interest in mining the deep sea. Because relatively little is known about many underwater ecosystems, marine conservationists are worried about the potential impacts of seabed mining.

Chemical pollutants enter oceans from many sources. Agricultural runoff sends massive amounts of fertilizers, manure, and other chemicals into rivers and oceans. Other pollutants from agriculture, such as pesticides, can be directly toxic to the plants and animals of marine ecosystems.

Many kinds of chemicals enter the world's waterways and oceans. When people improperly dispose of leftover medications, those drugs can negatively affect ocean life. The chemicals in some sunscreens, such as oxybenzone and octinoxate, wash off people's skin, enter the water, and can be absorbed by plants and animals. Large-scale oil spills, many from oil tankers, represent a major source of chemical pollution. Animals can become trapped in oil, inhale it accidentally, or be poisoned by eating it. The largest oil spills, such as the 2010 *Deepwater Horizon* spill in the Gulf of Mexico, occur when oil-drilling platforms explode or sink.

SHALLOW-WATER ECOSYSTEM THREATS

Coastal ecosystems are the most strongly affected by pollution. These include wetlands, salt marshes, mudflats, mangrove forests, seagrass beds, bays, estuaries, coral reefs, sponge reefs, and kelp forests. Pollution and other environmental dangers have harmed these places greatly. As a result, scientists have coined the term *coastal syndrome* to describe this damage to coastal ecosystems.

Construction projects are destroying many coastal ecosystems, including the salt marshes and reed beds of San Francisco Bay in California. The bay contains the largest wetland on the western coast of the United States. But about 90 percent of the wetland

Deepwater Horizon

On April 10, 2010, an oil rig in the Gulf of Mexico known as *Deepwater Horizon* exploded and sank. Around 134 million gallons (507 million L) of oil spilled into the ocean over the course of 87 days.[2] Scientists estimate around 82,000 birds, 6,000 sea turtles, and 26,000 marine mammals may have been harmed by the oil spill.[3] Other animals, including fish, coral, lobster, and sea stars, were also greatly affected. *Deepwater Horizon* is considered the largest offshore oil spill in history.

has been degraded or lost, mostly due to residential and industrial development.[4]

Coastal construction projects, such as seawalls intended to prevent coastal erosion, have affected similar ecosystems around the world. The building of seawalls in Canada, Europe, and South Korea has damaged bays and mudflats, which provide nesting areas for aquatic birds. Several bird populations have declined severely since the construction of these seawalls.

Tropical and subtropical mangrove forests are among the most important and most endangered coastal habitats. Mangroves are the only tree species able to grow in seawater because of their ability to take in more oxygen and to remove salt from the water they absorb. Their submerged roots form an important habitat for many animals, especially young fish.

Mangroves also protect coasts from storms by reducing the strength of incoming waves. But around the world, mangrove swamps are being drained and filled to provide land for harbors, hotels, and other projects. In Ecuador, up to 70 percent of mangrove swamps have been destroyed to build shrimp farms.[5]

Several coastal areas around the world are threatened by multiple factors at once. One of these areas is the Gulf of Mexico, which made the news for months in 2010 because of the *Deepwater Horizon* oil spill. But the Gulf also suffers from the ongoing problem of eutrophication.

The size of the Gulf of Mexico dead zone changes over time, but it can be as large as 7,000 square miles (18,100 sq km).[6]

The Gulf receives a constant overload of nutrients from agricultural and urban runoff from the Mississippi River. This results in algal blooms and oxygen depletion in a large region around the mouth of the river. Eutrophication kills the organisms in an area, forming what is known as a dead zone. The Gulf of Mexico contains the second-largest dead zone in the world. The largest is in the Gulf of Oman in the Arabian Sea.

Another highly threatened region is Australia's Great
Barrier Reef. It was designated a World Heritage Area by the
UN Educational, Scientific, and Cultural Organization (UNESCO)
in 1981. The Great Barrier Reef's diverse and beautiful coral reefs
and seagrass beds are home to many endangered species. They
are also a popular tourist site. But the reef is endangered due
to warming seas, eutrophication, coastal development, and
illegal fishing. The heat has caused intense coral bleaching, and
pollution is endangering both reefs and seagrasses.

OPEN-OCEAN AND DEEP-OCEAN THREATS

For hundreds of years, people have used the oceans as a
dumping ground for waste, both physical and chemical. Waste
from shore includes dredged
materials, mining waste,
industrial waste, and ash from
power stations. Much of the
material is toxic.

Waste accumulation often
destroys entire ecosystems,
damages the health of humans
and marine organisms, and
causes economic harm. The
oceans are so large that people may assume waste dumped far
from shore would be harmless. But because ocean currents carry
pollutants, the damage is not restricted to the dumping ground.

> " The ocean is not a dumping
> ground. . . . While we can
> forgive previous generations
> for not fully recognizing the
> importance of a clean ocean
> for life on this planet, there
> is no excuse today.[7] "
>
> —*Sylvia Earle, marine
> conservationist and
> ocean explorer, 2020*

About 20 percent of ocean waste comes from activities on the ocean itself.[8] These include shipping, energy extraction, mining, and tourism. All these activities involve ships, and these vessels produce a variety of pollution. Types of pollution from ships include oil and gas. These pollutants can leak during travel and in port as well as release sewage, garbage, and exhaust gases. Energy-extraction activities, such as drilling at oil rigs and shipping by oil tankers, can lead to oil spills. Mining activities can also release toxic chemicals into the water.

OTHER SOURCES OF POLLUTION

Another source of ocean pollution is noise pollution. Noise pollution is excess sound that comes from human activity and often disrupts marine life. The noise can come from the coast, shallow water, or the deep ocean. Noise pollution can harm all types of organisms, from plankton to whales.

Many marine animals, especially mammals, rely on certain adaptations to help them navigate, communicate, and hunt underwater. For example, dolphins produce sounds that bounce off the bodies of other animals to help them search for food. This is known as echolocation. However, ocean noise can disrupt these adaptations, making it difficult for the animals to do their natural behaviors.

Some of the major sources of ocean noise include shipping, piledriving, and seismic activity. Shipping is one of the most disruptive forms of ocean noise pollution. Around 90 percent of all global trades are now shipped by sea.[9] The sounds that come from ships, especially in areas with high levels of traffic, often prevent animals from being able to communicate with one another.

Seismic activity includes using air guns to search for oil and gas underwater. These air guns emit a very loud sound that can sometimes travel thousands of feet into the ocean. This sound can push animals out of their habitats and prevent them from breeding or feeding properly.

Piledriving is a form of construction in which foundations for bridges or offshore wind turbines are hammered into the seafloor. The hammering sounds can cause stress to animals or push migrating animals off their normal course. Some other sources of noise pollution include sonar used by militaries and deep-sea mining.

PROTECTING OCEANS FROM POLLUTION

Philip Landrigan of Boston College was the lead author of a 2020 study on ocean health. He says ocean pollution can be controlled with laws, technology, and enforcement targeting the main sources of pollution. The authors of the study called for the elimination of coal burning and for transitioning from fossil fuels to renewable energy sources. They recommended banning single-use plastics, controlling coastal pollution, and increasing the number of marine protected areas to safeguard

There are many ways to clean up after an oil spill. From the shore, oil can be suctioned from water using vacuums.

vulnerable ecosystems. The authors also recommended more community involvement and more research to better understand the health effects of ocean pollution, especially on humans.

One of the most valuable ocean protections enacted so far is the Ocean Dumping Act. Congress originally passed the Ocean Dumping Act in 1972 and amended the law in 1988. The act prohibits the transport and dumping of materials from anywhere inside or outside the United States into the ocean.

Exceptions are made with permits based on whether the dumping will "unreasonably degrade or endanger human health, welfare, or the marine environment."[11] The 1988 amendment of the Ocean Dumping Act further prohibits ocean dumping of municipal sewage sludge and industrial waste, including medical waste. The EPA enforces the act through its Ocean Dumping Management program.

Tuna, salmon, and cod are the most commonly eaten fish around the world.

CHAPTER 7

THE DECLINE OF OCEAN FISHERIES

Seafood provides a major source of protein for more than three billion people worldwide. But in 2023, about one-third of the world's fisheries were overfished, meaning they were being fished more rapidly than reproduction could replenish the populations of fish and other marine species.[1] Overfishing can result from poor management of fish populations, insufficient rules around fishing, or a lack of rules entirely.

A key factor in managing fish stocks is knowing when a stock is sustainable and when it is being overfished. A sustainable fishery can be fished without harming its overall population levels. That is, it is being fished at or below its maximum sustainable yield (MSY).

A stock being harvested at a rate greater than its MSY is being overfished. The stock's population size can decrease to the point where it can no longer replenish itself. Under proper management, a previously overfished stock can be rebuilt. When fisheries in the United States start to become overfished, NOAA Fisheries limits or halts fishing and tries to rebuild the population.

THE STATUS OF US AND WORLD FISHERIES

Worldwide, fishery stocks are facing challenges. In the last 50 years, fish and seafood production has quadrupled. Since the 1980s, the number of fish stocks being overexploited has more than doubled. And aquaculture production has increased 50 times from what it was in 1960 to what was produced in 2015.[2]

According to the UN Food and Agriculture Organization, 123 million short tons (112 million metric tons) of fish were harvested in marine waters in 2020, 70 percent from catching wild fish and 30 percent from aquaculture. About 89 percent of it was consumed by humans.[3] The remainder was mainly used to produce fish oil and fish meal.

However, world fish stocks are becoming less sustainable. In 1974, 90 percent of stocks were being fished at sustainable levels. By 2019, this percentage dropped to about 65 percent.[4] The waters of Europe and

Sharks are often accidentally caught in fishing nets. Although the sharks may be released back into the wild, many will still die due to injuries or stress.

the Mediterranean are particularly threatened by overfishing. In the Northeast Atlantic, more than 40 percent of fish stocks are overfished. In the Mediterranean, this figure is 90 percent.[5]

Rebecca Hubbard is the program director of the organization Our Fish, which works to end overfishing. She found that overfishing has caused many issues, including the degradation of marine ecosystems and the lowering of the ocean's ability to store carbon. "We are already seeing huge declines in populations of historically important fish, such as cod and herring, in many seas throughout Europe," says Hubbard. "In the Baltic Sea we are seeing ecosystems collapse from chronic overfishing combined with the effects of pollution and increasingly, warmer waters, which has led to many fishers dropping out of the industry."[6] Hubbard notes that to fix the issue of overfishing, world leaders need to better understand how it affects the ocean's natural ability to maintain marine ecosystems.

Fishing is a major industry in the United States. In 2020, it provided 1.7 million jobs and $253 billion in sales, with 61 percent of that coming from commercial fisheries.[7] NOAA Fisheries maintains US commercial fisheries by developing management plans, managing fish stocks, and collecting data to determine the status of each stock. NOAA's work is supported by the MSA, which is the major law regulating US fisheries.

Maintaining sustainable fisheries is a never-ending process. Strides have been made, but nearly 20 percent of fish stocks in the United States remained overfished in 2022.[8] These include the chronically overfished Atlantic cod and the Atlantic herring, an important prey fish. Many fish stocks have been rebuilt, but others are struggling to recover and need better management plans.

Some rebuilt stocks are becoming overfished again. Among these is the bluefish, an important fish species for recreational fishing. The National Resources Defense Council recognizes recent advances in US fisheries management but notes that climate change is slowing or even reversing that progress.

MODERN FISHING METHODS

The various methods for catching fish have differing effects on fish populations and the environment. Some fisheries are small scale, feeding only local communities. They are often found in developing countries and among Indigenous people. Methods include pole-and-line fishing, gillnets, and longlines.

Pole-and-line fishing catches fish one at a time. People will sometimes scatter bait fish on the surface to catch larger fish. This method is sustainable, resulting in low bycatch.

A gillnet is a net curtain that hangs in the water without touching the seabed. The size of the fish caught depends on the size of the net. Bycatch is greater because the gillnet does not target specific species. Longlines are long nets trailing behind a boat and fitted with baited hooks that target certain species. They are used for midwater and sometimes bottom fishing.

Purse seines and trawls are commonly used in large commercial fisheries. Purse seines surround a large single-species

A Law to Keep Fishing Sustainable

The Magnuson-Stevens Fishery Conservation and Management Act (MSA) first passed in 1976. Its major goal is to maintain sustainable fisheries in US federal waters. To do this, the MSA sets several objectives, which include preventing overfishing, rebuilding overfished stocks, and protecting habitats where fish spawn, breed, and grow. In this way, the act was intended to ensure a reliable seafood supply and maintain the social and economic benefits of fishing. In 2007, the MSA added yearly catch limits and strengthened international cooperation.

Midwater trawling mostly occurs in the ocean, but it can also be done in lakes.

school of fish, such as tuna or mackerel, and then draw the purse's strings together to capture the fish. The bycatch tends to be low for purse seines because specific schools of fish are being targeted.

Trawls are cone-shaped and closed at one end. Since they are dragged through the water on or just above the seabed, trawls are very efficient tools in terms of fish catch. However, they may have higher levels of bycatch because they aren't targeting one specific species.

Other methods include bottom trawls and dredges. Bottom trawling involves dragging a net along the seafloor, which can cause damage to the ecosystem. Dredging, which involves dragging a rigid structure along the seabed, is even more damaging because it digs deep into the seafloor. Hydraulic dredging greatly harms the environment, digging 6.3 inches (16 cm) into the seafloor and killing about 41 percent of the organisms in its path.[10] Pots and traps made from wire, wood, or plastic are often left on the seabed for up to 24 hours and used to catch lobsters and crabs.

Bottom trawling accounts for about 25 percent of the world fish catch, and midwater trawling makes up another 10 percent. Purse seines account for approximately 20 percent of the world fish catch. Because gillnets and longlines capture fewer fish at a time, they contribute a much lower percentage.

Bottom trawling is the most common method used in China and India, and its usage continues to rise. This fishing style is becoming much less common in Europe as countries there try to decrease overfishing and rebuild their stocks. In 2016, the European Commission banned trawling in waters less than 2,625 feet (800 m) deep.[11]

DEEP-SEA FISHERIES

Outside the coastal areas and the continental shelf, the ocean slopes down and drops off abruptly into the deep sea. This vast region is not just a flat plain but contains banks, ridges, and underwater mountains known as seamounts. Life in these areas, including in deep-water coral reefs and ecosystems around deep hydrothermal vents, is diverse. Seamounts have large, complex ecosystems.

The deep sea was not commercially fished until the 1950s, when refrigerated ships suited for deep-sea fishing first became available. In the 1970s, the Soviet Union and Japan specialized in deep-sea fishing. By 2008, 27 countries were involved in this method of fishing. Early catches around seamounts and banks were huge. But the fishers used trawls, which destroyed the ocean floor. Many species were quickly decimated.

Deep-sea species often reproduce slowly, having fewer offspring and longer lifespans. For example, the deep-sea orange roughy fish achieves sexual maturity at age 25 and lives to be 125. This makes deep-sea species especially vulnerable to overfishing. Deep-sea fishing poses a huge threat to ocean environments.

SOLUTIONS FOR SUSTAINABLE FISHERIES

The Marine Stewardship Council (MSC) is an international organization that raises awareness about the dangers of overfishing and promotes sustainable fishing practices.

When measuring sustainability, the MSC considers three principles. These are maintaining sustainable fish stocks, minimizing environmental impacts, and practicing effective management. After a fishery is MSC certified, it is reassessed periodically to ensure it is applying the latest scientific knowledge to maintain sustainable practices. The MSC's goal is to preserve fisheries for future generations.

Agreements between governments in developed and developing nations can be a partial solution to fishery problems. Under such agreements, developed nations work with developing nations to improve fishing practices. This can help protect marine ecosystems while providing the fish protein needed to sustain human health and livelihoods.

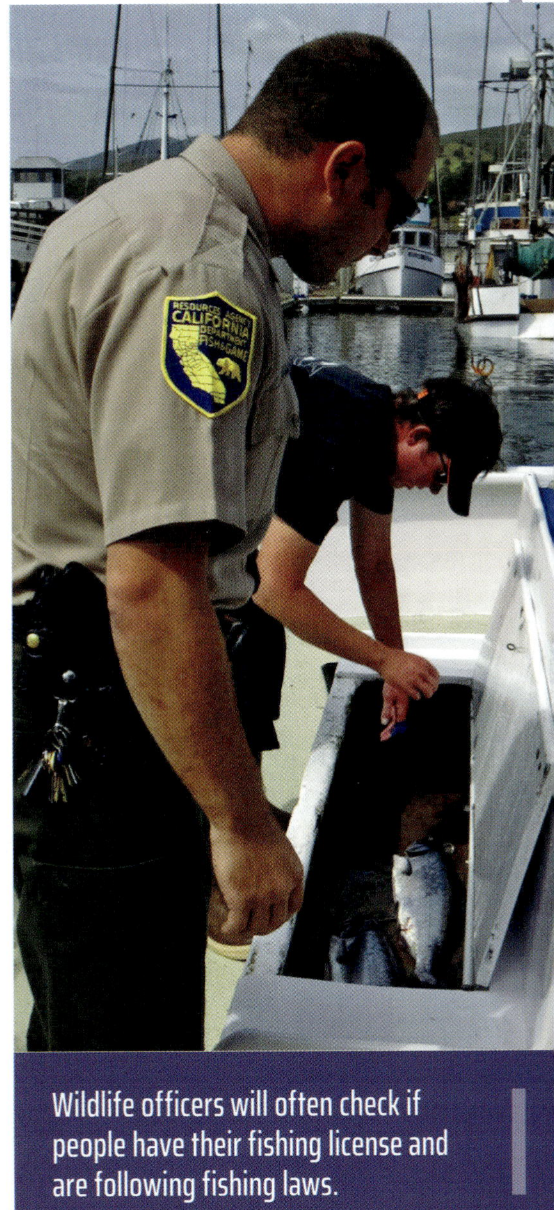

Wildlife officers will often check if people have their fishing license and are following fishing laws.

One type of sustainable management involves a system known as fishing rights. In this system, individuals, companies, or communities are given the right to fish in a particular location as long as they follow certain catch limits and regulations. These individuals and groups are often given incentives to follow the regulations to help maintain the health of fish populations. This method has worked in countries such as Belize, Denmark, Namibia, and the United States, among others.

In 1982, the UN Convention on the Law of the Sea established the idea of exclusive economic zones (EEZs). EEZs are areas extending 230 miles (370 km) from a nation's coast where the nation has the rights to use the resources of the sea and the ocean floor.[13] This includes through activities such as fishing and mining.

> We need governments to shift from thinking that fishing is just about one small industry that provides food to people . . . to seeing fishing as a critical impact to be holistically managed in order to maintain planetary health for all.[14]
>
> —Rebecca Hubbard, program director of Our Fish, 2022

Foreign governments can negotiate and pay for the right to fish within another nation's EEZs. This can help nations manage conservation in these areas, although some commercial fishers still fish illegally. Another solution is to set up areas where fishing is prohibited, such as no-take zones and marine reserves. These areas help replenish fish stocks and support sustainable fisheries.

People who catch lobsters must measure the animals to make sure they aren't too big or small. Any lobsters that don't fit the measurements are released back into the sea.

But not all solutions to reduce or prevent overfishing involve governments. The seafood industry is market driven, meaning it is often influenced by the needs and wants of customers. Informed consumers can have a great influence on the health of ecosystems and the threat of overfishing. If consumers demand sustainably produced fish products, it is more likely the seafood industry will provide them. In short, there are several ways to maintain sustainable fisheries, and many of them are already being tested.

People interested in marine conservation can volunteer to help release animals such as sea turtles into the wild.

GETTING INVOLVED IN MARINE CONSERVATION

Every person, regardless of location, can find ways to protect Earth's oceans and marine organisms. Activist Greta Thunberg explains, "Protecting the ocean is not just about saving marine life; it's about safeguarding our own future."[1] Protecting oceans can be as simple or as involved as each person chooses.

Taking action to protect oceans can mean giving money, joining an organization, or making changes in one's everyday life. It could mean staying informed and informing others whenever possible. For some, it might even mean going to college to become a professional marine conservationist.

STARTING SMALL

An ocean-conscious person will think about how their life affects oceans and will then act accordingly. The easiest and most immediate ways to get involved in marine conservation can begin at home. Making changes in one's lifestyle is a simple first step. This includes decreasing plastic use and eating only sustainably caught seafood. It also includes participating in cleanup efforts such as picking up litter and reducing one's personal waste and energy use.

Staying up to date on marine conservation news by reading books, news stories, and social media is a great way to stay informed. Watching documentaries can help people visualize the challenges of ocean conservation. Sharing information with friends and family will help spread the word and make more people conscious of the need for conservation efforts.

In addition to staying informed, a person interested in marine conservation might begin to inform others. They could find

Sustainable fishing practices are one way people can help protect oceans and marine species.

opportunities to speak publicly or write articles about marine conservation, post about marine conservation issues on social media, or produce a blog. Even without formal education in marine conservation, an informed person can educate others about how people can damage oceans and how everyone is responsible for ocean conservation.

VOLUNTEERS AND INTERNS

Volunteer organizations and nongovernmental organizations are always looking for members and volunteers. Some prominent examples include the Marine Conservation Institute, the Ocean Conservancy, the Ocean Conservation Trust, the Marine Conservation Society, and Oceana. People who want to get involved can learn about each organization and join the one that is most in-line with their interests.

Organizations will provide information about their programs to people who join. They may also ask members to get involved by signing petitions. In addition, organizations may have programs that set volunteers to work doing things such as collecting water samples or protecting sea turtle eggs.

Internships are especially valuable for those who hope to become professional marine conservationists. They are available from academic institutions and conservation organizations around the globe. They may be paid or unpaid. These positions can help people learn more about a particular aspect of marine conservation without having a science degree. Some internships even offer academic credit.

There are also many ways to contribute to marine conservation that do not directly involve science. People can get involved in internships that emphasize communications, science policy, business, or other marine conservation–related areas. For anyone who hopes to enter the marine conservation field, both volunteer work and internships are valuable ways to gain experience.

In 2022, volunteers at NOAA's National Marine Sanctuaries contributed 57,223 hours of their time. That is equivalent to the hours of 31 full-time employees.[2]

Some people may take a trip centered on a marine conservation project. These kinds of trips can be expensive. But they may involve projects suited to a wide variety of interests related to conservation.

Volunteers can even become citizen scientists. Citizen scientists are members of the public who are directed by scientists to collect data or do work that contributes to scientific research, conservation efforts, and sustainable practices.

The organization Global Vision International, for example, conducts projects to restore coral reefs, monitor marine animal populations, rehabilitate sea turtles and hatchlings, tag sharks, and survey biodiversity in coral reefs and seagrass beds.

GETTING SERIOUS ABOUT OCEANS

Some people may want to make ocean conservation their life's work. There are many ways to accomplish this, not all of which involve working directly in oceans. People can get jobs related to marine animal care, communication and marketing, community outreach, fundraising, photography and filmmaking, marine management, and more.

Some of these positions may involve specialized training, including college degrees. But most do not require degrees in marine biology or marine conservation specifically. For those interested in marine conservation jobs, it is always good preparation to learn skills useful for one's areas of interest, such as swimming, scuba diving, or photography.

Those who want to go specifically into marine conservation often begin with a degree in marine biology. Studying marine biology can involve a variety of specializations, such as the behavior of marine species or the effects of human activities on marine ecosystems. There are even degrees related to fishery management.

With a bachelor's or master's degree, a marine conservationist can work as a research assistant at a university or college or as a scientist at a private or government organization. Those with PhDs can become university professors or professional researchers. Given the effects of climate change on oceans, marine conservationists may also work on climate-related projects, so learning about climate change can be useful for these careers.

LOOKING BEYOND THE PERSONAL

Individual actions are important to marine conservation, but laws and regulations must also be in place to protect the planet's oceans. Because most ocean

Marine biologists may go out on boats to collect data on marine species or habitats.

Workers at zoos and aquariums will clean and rehabilitate animals that have been caught in oil spills.

waters do not fall under the jurisdiction of any country, there has always been some confusion and dispute over who owns the sea's resources and how they should be managed. The 1982 UN Convention on the Law of the Sea established rules outlining management of the sea and its resources.

Among other things, the Law of the Sea specifies laws and regulations prohibiting the release of plastics, toxins, and other pollutants into the ocean. By 2022, 158 countries had signed and ratified it.[4] Several other countries, including the United States, have signed but not ratified it. Ratification means adoption of the treaty's laws as national laws.

In March 2023, the UN reached a new agreement to protect biodiversity in international waters. This agreement protects certain areas of the high seas, regions more than 230 miles (370 km) offshore, which are outside national waters and comprise two-thirds of the ocean.[5] In addition to high seas protected areas, the agreement mandates funding for marine conservation.

> Far and away the greatest threat to the oceans . . . is ignorance. But we can do something about that.[6]
>
> —Sylvia Earle, marine conservationist and ocean explorer, 2017

Lack of funding, knowledge, personnel, and technology hamper marine conservation efforts in developing countries. In developed countries, problems include lack of cooperation, conflicting goals, and maximizing profits at the expense of the marine environment. To solve the increasingly severe problems of climate change, ocean pollution, and decreased ocean biodiversity, government regulations and policies need to be put in place.

However, it is also important to make decisions about marine conservation on a scientific basis while always considering the interests of local and Indigenous communities. Efforts to improve marine conservation will take hard work and cooperation from all countries and organizations to turn things around. It will also require the committed actions of all people on Earth.

MARINE CONSERVATION PROBLEMS

- Climate change is endangering marine organisms and environments by raising ocean temperatures, increasing ocean acidity, causing more intense storms, and raising sea levels around the world.

- Plastics are among the major pollutants entering oceans. Animals ingest plastics instead of food, which may cause them to die of starvation. They can also become tangled in nets and drown if they can't escape. Most plastic pollution consists of single-use items such as plastic bags, cups, and straws.

- Coastal activities send many kinds of chemical pollutants into coastal oceans and bays. These include sewage and nutrients from fertilizers. Pollutants can cause harmful algal growth, resulting in reduced oxygen levels that kill off marine life. Toxic industrial pollutants can damage or destroy marine ecosystems.

- More than three billion people depend on world fisheries for seafood. However, many fisheries are being overfished, and some have become unsustainable.

- Overfishing is causing a decline in fish populations and ocean biodiversity.

MARINE CONSERVATION SOLUTIONS

- Passing laws such as the Ocean Dumping Act to prevent toxic materials from being dumped into the ocean.

- Setting regulations on individuals and fisheries to prevent overfishing in more sensitive environments and maintain the sustainability of fish populations.

- Creating marine protected areas to help preserve fragile and ecologically important habitats around the world.

- Restoring marine ecosystems, including mangroves, seagrass beds, and coral reefs, to support ocean wildlife and coastal communities.

TAKING ACTION

- Stay informed on threats to oceans and marine life and help educate others on those issues.

- Avoid the use of single-use plastics and participate in beach and river cleanups to prevent trash from entering the world's oceans.

- Dispose of harmful chemicals safely and properly to prevent them from polluting the ocean and harming marine life.

- Promote laws and regulations that will help maintain and restore marine environments.

QUOTE

"What happens to the ocean impacts all of us."

—Janis Searles Jones, chief executive officer of the Ocean Conservancy

aquaculture
The process of raising fish and other aquatic animals for food.

aquifer
An underground rock formation that contains water or allows water to flow through.

atmosphere
The layer of gases surrounding a planet.

biodiversity
The many different plants and animals in an ecosystem.

deforestation
The action of clearing a large group of trees.

degrade
To reduce a habitat's quality.

ecosystem
A community of interacting organisms and their environment.

glacier
A large, thickened mass of ice formed from fallen snow that has compacted and been added to over many years.

greenhouse gas (GHG)
A gas such as carbon dioxide or methane that absorbs infrared radiation and traps heat in the atmosphere.

gyre
A large system of circulating surface currents in the ocean.

interdisciplinary
Using more than one branch of science to study something.

invertebrate
An animal without a spinal column.

jurisdiction
A certain area within which a group has authority to make a legal decision or take legal action.

migration
The seasonal behavior in which a group of animals travels relatively long distances between locations, usually to escape unfavorable conditions or to find food.

pollutant
A substance that is harmful to the environment.

submersible
A small vehicle that can operate underwater, used especially for research.

sustainable
A practice that avoids depleting natural resources.

toxic
Poisonous to an animal or habitat.

wetland
An area where the land is saturated with water.

SELECTED BIBLIOGRAPHY

Ritchie, Hannah and Max Roser. "Fish and Overfishing." *Our World in Data*, Oct. 2021, ourworldindata.org. Accessed 27 Oct. 2023.

"The Great Pacific Garbage Patch." *Ocean Cleanup*, 2023, theoceancleanup.com. Accessed 27 Oct. 2023.

"The Ocean—The World's Greatest Ally against Climate Change." *United Nations*, n.d., un.org. Accessed 27 Oct. 2023.

FURTHER READINGS

Kaye, Cathryn Berger. *Going Blue: A Teen Guide to Saving Oceans, Lakes, Rivers & Wetlands*. Free Spirit, 2023.

Mooney, Carla. *Climate Change*. Abdo, 2025.

Nakaya, Andrea C. *Healthy Oceans: Why They Matter*. ReferencePoint, 2023.

Pêgo, Ana, and Isabel Minhós Martins. *Plasticus Maritimus: An Invasive Species*. Greystone Kids, 2020.

ONLINE RESOURCES

To learn more about marine conservation, please visit **abdobooklinks.com** or scan this QR code. These links are routinely monitored and updated to provide the most current information available.

MORE INFORMATION

For more information on this subject, contact or visit the following organizations:

National Oceanic and Atmospheric Administration Fisheries
1315 East-West Hwy., 14th Floor
Silver Spring, MD 20910
fisheries.noaa.gov
The National Oceanic and Atmospheric Administration (NOAA) Fisheries is a government agency within the US Department of Commerce that is responsible for overseeing marine resources in the United States. The website has information on protected species and ecosystem conservation.

Ocean Conservancy
1300 19th St. NW, 8th Floor
Washington, DC 20036
oceanconservancy.org
The Ocean Conservancy is a nonprofit organization that promotes healthy, diverse marine ecosystems and works to prevent and reduce threats to marine and human life.

Oceana
1025 Connecticut Ave., Ste. 200
Washington, DC 20036
oceana.org
Oceana is the world's largest advocacy foundation for ocean conservation. Its mission is to protect and restore the world's oceans.

CHAPTER 1. BECOMING AN OCEAN ADVOCATE

1. "Hawaiian Monk Seal." *National Oceanic and Atmospheric Administration Fisheries*, 12 Jan. 2024, fisheries.noaa.gov. Accessed 23 Jan. 2024.

2. Olivia Lai. "11 of the Most Endangered Species in the Ocean in 2024." *Earth.org*, 17 Jan. 2024, earth.org. Accessed 23 Jan. 2024.

3. "Ocean Conservancy's Vision." *Ocean Conservancy*, n.d., oceanconservancy.org. Accessed 23 Jan. 2024.

4. L. Rojas-Bracho, B.L. Taylor, and A. Jaramillo-Legotteta. "Vaquita." *International Union for Conservation of Nature Red List*, 2 Mar. 2022, iucnredlist.org. Accessed 23 Jan. 2024.

5. "New Estimate Finds North Atlantic Right Whale Population Still at Risk." *Oceana*, 23 Oct. 2023, usa.oceana.org. Accessed 23 Jan. 2024.

6. "Our Impact." *4ocean*, 2024, 4ocean.com. Accessed 23 Jan. 2024.

7. Tom Huddleston Jr. "These 20-Something Surfers Started a Company That's Pulled 1 Million Pounds of Garbage out of the Ocean." *CNBC*, 7 Sept. 2018, cnbc.com. Accessed 23 Jan. 2024.

CHAPTER 2. THE SCIENCE OF MARINE CONSERVATION

1. "How Much Water Is in the Ocean?" *National Oceanic and Atmospheric Administration*, 5 June 2023, oceanservice.noaa.gov. Accessed 23 Jan. 2024.

2. Carl Safina. "Launching a Sea Ethic." *Wild Earth*, Winter 2002/2003, p. 5, environmentandsociety.org. Accessed 23 Jan. 2024.

3. John Dos Passos Coggin. "A Conversation with Polar Oceanographer Rebecca Jackson." *Climate.gov*, 9 Feb. 2021, climate.gov. Accessed 23 Jan. 2024.

4. Ayesha Tandon. "Melting Drove '21% of Sea Level Rise' Over Past Two Decades." *CarbonBrief*, 28 Apr. 2021, carbonbrief.org. Accessed 23 Jan. 2024.

5. "What Is Climate Change?" *National Aeronautics and Space Administration*, n.d. climate.nasa.gov. Accessed 23 Jan. 2024.

6. Eirini Kardara. "Global Warming/Climate Change/Ocean Acidification." *MarineBio Conservation Society*, n.d., marinebio.org. Accessed 23 Jan. 2024.

7. Jon Marcus. "Hawaiian Coral Evolution Sparks Worldwide Debate." *Times Higher Education*, 13 Feb. 2016, timeshighereducation.com. Accessed 23 Jan. 2024.

8. Marta Fava. "The Threats to the Ocean in 2022 and How to Prevent Them." *United Nations Educational, Scientific and Cultural Organization*, 9 May 2022, oceanliteracy.unesco.org. Accessed 23 Jan. 2024.

9. "Dumping by the Numbers." *Earthworks*, 22 Feb. 2018, earthworks.org. Accessed 23 Jan. 2024.

CHAPTER 3. THE HISTORY OF MARINE CONSERVATION

1. "A History of the Study of Marine Biology." *MarineBio Conservation Society*, n.d., marinebio.org. Accessed 23 Jan. 2024.

2. "A History of Marine Biology."

3. "A History of Marine Biology."

4. "EPA History: Marine Protection, Research and Sanctuaries Act (Ocean Dumping Act)." *Environmental Protection Agency*, 7 June 2023, epa.gov. Accessed 23 Jan. 2024.

5. "Laws & Policies: Endangered Species Act." *National Oceanic and Atmospheric Administration Fisheries*, n.d., fisheries.noaa.gov. Accessed 23 Jan. 2024.

6. "Summary Report, 3–9 February 2023: 5th International Marine Protected Areas Congress (IMPAC5)." *International Institute for Sustainable Development*, 18 Feb. 2023, enb.iisd.org. Accessed 23 Jan. 2024.

7. Beth Pike. "A (Marine) Conservation Carol: A Visit from the Ghost of Conservation Past." *Marine Conservation Institute*, 12 Jan. 2021, marine-conservation.org. Accessed 23 Jan. 2024.

8. "Marine Protected Areas." *Protected Planet*, n.d., protectedplanet.net. Accessed 23 Jan. 2024.

9. "Global Marine Protection Agreements." *Marine Conservation Institute*, n.d., old.mpatlas.org. Accessed 23 Jan. 2024.

10. "Understating Area-Based Management in U.S. Waters." *National Marine Protected Areas Center*, n.d., marineprotectedareas.noaa.gov. Accessed 23 Jan. 2024.

CHAPTER 4. OCEANS AND CLIMATE CHANGE

1. "How Is Climate Change Impacting the World's Ocean." *United Nations*, n.d., un.org. Accessed 23 Jan. 2024.

2. Alejandra Borunda. "Why Are Our Oceans Getting Warmer?" *National Geographic*, 1 May 2023, nationalgeographic.com. Accessed 23 Jan. 2024.

3. "The Ongoing Marine Heat Waves in U.S. Waters, Explained." *National Oceanic and Atmospheric Administration*, 14 July 2023, noaa.gov. Accessed 23 Jan. 2024.

4. "Climate Change Impacting the World's Oceans."

5. "Marine Heat Waves in U.S."

6. Ilissa Ocko and Tianyi Sun. "How Climate Change Makes Hurricanes More Destructive." *Environmental Defense Fund*, n.d., edf.org. Accessed 23 Jan. 2024.

7. "Ocean Heat." *Environmental Protection Agency*, Aug. 2016, epa.gov. Accessed 23 Jan. 2024.

8. "Climate Change Indicators: Sea Surface Temperature." *Environmental Protection Agency*, April 2021, epa.gov. Accessed 9 Feb. 2024.

9. "Climate Change Impacting the World's Oceans."

10. Christina Nunez. "Sea Levels Are Rising at an Extraordinary Pace. Here's What to Know." *National Geographic*, 10 Apr. 2023, nationalgeographic.com. Accessed 23 Jan. 2024.

11. Rebecca Lindsey. "Climate Change: Global Sea Level Rise." *Climate.gov*, 19 Apr. 2022, climate.gov. Accessed 23 Jan. 2024.

12. "NASA Uses 30-Year Satellite Record to Track and Project Rising Seas." *National Aeronautics and Space Administration*, 17 Mar. 2023, climate.nasa.gov. Accessed 23 Jan. 2024.

13. Sally Younger. "NASA Study: Rising Sea Level Could Exceed Estimates for U.S. Coasts." *National Aeronautics and Space Administration*, 15 Nov. 2022, climate.nasa.gov. Accessed 23 Jan. 2024.

14. "Advancing NASA Sea Level Science and Interdisciplinary Research." *National Aeronautics and Space Administration Sea Level Change*, n.d., sealevel.nasa.gov. Accessed 23 Jan. 2024.

15. Eirini Kardara. "Global Warming/Climate Change/Ocean Acidification." *MarineBio Conservation Society*, n.d., marinebio.org. Accessed 23 Jan. 2024.

16. "Ocean Acidification." *National Oceanic and Atmospheric Administration*, 1 Apr. 2020, noaa.gov. Accessed 23 Jan. 2024.

17. "What You Need to Know about Oceans and Climate Change." *World Bank*, 8 Feb. 2022, worldbank.org. Accessed 23 Jan. 2024.

18. "The Ocean—The World's Greatest Ally against Climate Change." *United Nations*, n.d., un.org. Accessed 23 Jan. 2024.

CHAPTER 5. OCEAN PLASTICS

1. John Briley. "Confronting Ocean Plastic Pollution." *Pew*, 16 Nov. 2020, pewtrusts.org. Accessed 23 Jan. 2024.

2. "Ocean Plastics Pollution." *Center for Biological Diversity*, n.d., biologicaldiversity.org. Accessed 23 Jan. 2024.

3. "The Problem of Marine Plastic Pollution." *Clean Water Action*, n.d., cleanwater.org. Accessed 23 Jan. 2024.

4. "Marine Plastic Pollution."

5. "Ocean Plastics Pollution."

6. "Ocean Plastics Pollution."

7. "Ocean Plastics Pollution."

8. "Marine Microplastics." *Woods Hole Oceanographic Institution*, n.d., whoi.edu. Accessed 23 Jan. 2024.

9. "Marine Plastic Pollution."

10. "The Great Pacific Garbage Patch." *Ocean Cleanup*, n.d., theoceancleanup.com. Accessed 23 Jan. 2024.

11. "Plastic in Our Oceans Is Killing Marine Mammals." *World Wildlife Fund Australia*, 26 June 2023, wwf.org.au. Accessed 23 Jan. 2024.

12. "Great Pacific Garbage Patch."

13. "Founder and CEO: Boyan Slat." *Ocean Cleanup*, n.d., theoceancleanup.com. Accessed 23 Jan. 2024.

14. Ivana Kottasová. "The Great Pacific Garbage Patch Is Now So Huge and Permanent That a Coastal Ecosystem Is Thriving on It, Scientists Say." *CNN*, 18 Apr. 2023, cnn.com. Accessed 23 Jan. 2024.

15. Kottasová, "Great Pacific Garbage Patch."

16. Briley, "Confronting Ocean Plastic Pollution."

17. "7 Solutions to Ocean Plastic Pollution." *Oceanic Society*, 24 Feb. 2023, oceanicsociety.org. Accessed 23 Jan. 2024.

18. Andy Extance. "Taking Responsibility for Waste." *Chemistry World*, 28 Apr. 2020, chemistryworld.com. Accessed 23 Jan. 2024.

CHAPTER 6. POLLUTION IN OCEAN ECOSYSTEMS

1. "Deep-Sea Mining." *International Union for Conservation of Nature*, May 2022, iucn.org. Accessed 23 Jan. 2024.

2. "Deepwater Horizon." *National Oceanic and Atmospheric Administration*, 5 Oct. 2022, noaa.gov. Accessed 23 Jan. 2024.

3. "A Deadly Toll: The Devastating Wildlife Effects of *Deepwater Horizon*—and the Next Catastrophic Oil Spill." *Center for Biological Diversity*, n.d., biologicaldiversity.org. Accessed 23 Jan. 2024.

4. "Wetland Conservation and Protection." *San Francisco Baykeeper*, n.d. baykeeper.org. Accessed 23 Jan. 2024.

5. "The Hidden Cost of Farmed Shrimp from Ecuador." *ClientEarth*, 13 July 2023, clientearth.org. Accessed 23 Jan. 2024.

6. Monica Bruckner. "The Gulf of Mexico Dead Zone." *Science Education Resource Center at Carleton College*, n.d., serc.carleton.edu. Accessed 23 Jan. 2024.

7. Leila Mead. "'The Ocean Is Not a Dumping Ground' Fifty Years of Regulating Ocean Dumping." *International Institute for Sustainable Development*, 7 Dec. 2021, iisd.org. Accessed 23 Jan. 2024.

8. "Causes & Effects of Ocean Pollution: What Are the Sources?" *Inspire Clean Energy*, n.d., inspirecleanenergy.com. Accessed 23 Jan. 2024.

9. "Who Pollutes the Ocean with Noise?" *Ocean Care*, n.d., oceancare.org. Accessed 23 Jan. 2024.

10. Elizabeth Claire Alberts. "Keep It Down: U.N. Report Lists Ways to Reduce Ocean Noise Pollution." *Mongabay*, 6 July 2023, news.mongabay.com. Accessed 23 Jan. 2024.

11. "Summary of the Marine Protection, Research, and Sanctuaries Act." *Environmental Protection Agency*, 14 Dec. 2023, epa.gov. Accessed 23 Jan. 2024.

CHAPTER 7. THE DECLINE OF OCEAN FISHERIES

1. "Overfishing." *World Wildlife Fund*, n.d., worldwildlife.org. Accessed 23 Jan. 2024.

2. Hannah Ritchie and Max Roser. "Fish and Overfishing." *Our World in Data*, Oct. 2021, ourworldindata.org. Accessed 23 Jan. 2024.

3. "Global Fisheries and Aquaculture at a Glance." *Food and Agriculture Organization of the United Nations*, 2022, fao.org. Accessed 23 Jan. 2024.

4. "The Status of Fishery Resources." *Food and Agriculture Organization of the United Nations*, 2022, fao.org. Accessed 23 Jan. 2024.

5. "Plenty of Fish?" *United Nations Climate Change*, 10 June 2022, unfccc.int. Accessed 23 Jan. 2024.

6. "Plenty of Fish?"

7. "Fisheries Economics of the United States, 2020 Report." *National Oceanic and Atmospheric Administration Fisheries*, 17 Feb. 2023, fisheries.noaa.gov. Accessed 23 Jan. 2024.

8. "Status of Stocks 2022." *National Oceanic and Atmospheric Administration Fisheries*, 9 Aug. 2023, fisheries.noaa.gov. Accessed 9 Feb. 2024.

9. "Sustainable Fisheries." *MarineBio Conservation Society*, n.d., marinebio.org. Accessed 23 Jan. 2024.

10. Ritchie and Roser, "Fish and Overfishing."

11. Ritchie and Roser, "Fish and Overfishing."

12. "Stop Whaling." *Whale and Dolphin Conservation*, n.d., us.whales.org. Accessed 23 Jan. 2024.

13. "What Is the EEZ?" *National Oceanic and Atmospheric Administration Fisheries Ocean Exploration*, n.d., oceanexplorer.noaa.gov. Accessed 23 Jan. 2024.

14. "Plenty of Fish?"

CHAPTER 8. GETTING INVOLVED IN MARINE CONSERVATION

1. Branden Harvey. "74 Best Ocean Quotes to Inspire Awe & Care." *Good Good Good*, 5 June 2023, goodgoodgood.co. Accessed 23 Jan. 2024.

2. "Volunteer." *National Marine Sanctuaries*, n.d., sanctuaries.noaa.gov. Accessed 23 Jan. 2024.

3. Derrick Z. Jackson. "Off the Coast of Maine, Puffins Are Rebounding and Feasting on a New Snack." *Maine Monitor*, 30 Aug. 2023, themainemonitor.org. Accessed 23 Jan. 2024.

4. Shanthi Van Zeebroeck. "Marine Conservation in International Law." *Earth.org*, 4 July 2022, earth.org. Accessed 23 Jan. 2024.

5. Kelsey Simpkins. "Historic High Seas Treaty Brings New Hope to Global Marine Conservation." *University of Colorado Boulder*, 10 Mar. 2023, colorado.edu. Accessed 23 Jan. 2024.

6. Sylvia A. Earle (@SylviaEarle). 2017. "Far and away, the greatest threat to the ocean, and thus to ourselves, is ignorance. But we can do something about that." *X*, 22 Aug. 2017, twitter.com. Accessed 23 Jan. 2024.

CAROL HAND

Carol Hand has a PhD in zoology with a specialization in marine ecology and a special interest in environmental and climate science. Before becoming a science writer, she taught college courses, wrote for standardized testing companies, and developed multimedia science curricula. She has written more than 60 educational books for young people on science and other topics. More recently, she has turned to fiction and has written (as C. S. Hand) three books in a young adult science fiction series, *Sam and Jade's Alien Adventures*. These sci-fi adventures also have an environmental theme.